Come, Sit in My Presence

A Daily Devotional

Rosalind Renshaw

A.S.K. Publishing
Bellevue, Washington
2001

Come, Sit in My Presence

International Standard Book Number 0-9671887-2-5

Published by: A.S.K. Publishing
P.O. Box 522
Bellevue, WA 98009

Ask, and it will be given you;
Search, and you will find;
Knock, and the door will be opened for you.
Matthew 7:7

Printed in the United States by:
Morris Publishing
3212 East Highway 30
Kearney, NE 68847
1-800-650-7888

Come, Sit in My Presence

A Daily Devotional

To Theresa

Love and Blessings!
Rosalind Renshaw

Romans 15:13

Christmas 2001

Dear Reader,

 "Come, Sit in My Presence" is God's invitation to you to spend time with him each day. God knows how busy we are – how fragmented and frenzied our lives have become. God longs for us to make space and time for him in our lives. He wants us to slow down so that we can hear his voice speaking to us every day.

I'm excited to offer you these "prayer-poems" as a daily devotional. Whether you are quiet before God first thing in the morning, at night, or somewhere in between, I hope these prayers help you come into God's presence. God loves you more than anyone else you will ever meet! God wants to communicate with you, hear from you, and give you his perspective and input on your life.

I still find it difficult to have a regular time and place to sit and talk with God. I do best when I sit with paper and pen, intentionally listening for God to speak to me. When he speaks, I record what I hear, and that is how these prayers are created. Sometimes I feel the nudge of the Holy Spirit and I ask for a poem on a specific theme. I know that setting aside a special place and time to meet with God is the best way to develop this life-giving and life-changing discipline.

Each devotion has a conversation with God, followed by a Scripture. As you read both, and meditate upon them, ask the Holy Spirit to speak directly to you. Try reading them more than once, and then write down what you hear God saying to you. You'll find additional Scriptures at the end of the book that you can refer to and reflect on.

My hope is that you will increasingly find joy as you spend daily time with God; and that what may have been a burden or a duty before, will become a source of strength and peace for you. My prayer is that the Holy Spirit will speak to you through these devotionals and that your faith will be renewed and deepened. For any of you who don't yet know the love of God expressed by his Son, Jesus Christ, it is my prayer that God will use these conversations to introduce you to him.

Rosalind Renshaw
September, 2001

Acknowledgements

My heartfelt thanks to God and to the friends who have made this book possible: Carol McKinstry my partner in this ministry, who supports and helps me in countless ways; Jenny Burritt, who prepared the manuscript for publication; Ross Candoo, who took my photograph; and my gratitude to all those who responded positively to my first book, "Conversations," and to the CD, and then asked when my next book would be available!

This book is lovingly dedicated to:
Rebecca and Matthew,
my beloved children.
You are precious gifts from God to me.
Thank you for all the love and joy you
bring into my life!

Come, Sit in My Presence

Frantic Pace

Life rushes by
at a frantic pace
Do I ever stop long enough
to taste your grace?
Or even pause for a moment
to catch a glimpse of your face?
My life's rushing by
at such a frantic pace

Lord, help me to slow down
so that I can see your face
Lord, help me to take the time
so that I can taste your grace
Lord, please help me to stop
and spend time with you
Please help me, Lord
I want to know you

The Lord bless you and keep you;
the Lord make his face to shine upon you,
and be gracious to you;
the Lord lift up his countenance upon you,
and give you peace.

Numbers 6:24-26

Be Still and Know That I Am God

Lord, I find it so hard to be still, even to slow down
let alone stop, and cease activity
I find it hard to relax, to allow myself to rest,
to invite you to re-create me
and yet I hear your gentle voice inviting me
to enter into your rhythm of life and living,
of love and loving
where I will find rest, and refreshment
relaxation, relief, re-creation, and release

Lord, please help me to know in my heart and head
that you are God - I am not
that you are in control of me,
my life, the world, the cosmos
I do not have to be in charge

Free me from the compulsion
to need to be in control of all things at all times
I am not God - you are

Teach me, Lord, how to relax and rejoice in that truth
and help me to allow myself
times of quiet and tranquility
times of silence and serenity
pools of peace in the midst of my days
where I can visit with you and get quiet enough,
inside and out
to hear your voice calling my name
speaking to me your words of love:

> You are my beloved, my precious one
> I love you, I always have, and I always will

Believe me
Let the words soak deeply into your heart and mind
I love you
Don't protest in disbelief
I do know you, through and through
and yes, I do love you even so
I long for you to respond to my love more fully,
more freely
To invite me into every part of your life
To sit with me each day and visit
I am God
You are my beloved child
I made you to be loved by me, and by many others
Open up your heart and let my love flow in
and then let it flow on out
to everyone you meet in my circle of life and love
My child, this day
be still, and know that I am God!

The Lord is good to those who wait for him,
to the soul that seeks him.
It is good that one should wait quietly
for the salvation of the Lord.

Lamentations 3:25-26

Come, Sit in My Presence

Come, sit in my presence
Don't say a word
Now is the time for my voice
Not yours, to be heard

Come, sit in the silence
Soak it into your heart
Let go of your striving
Which keeps us apart

Come, sit in my presence
I'm right here with you
I'm closer than breathing
Don't doubt that it's true

Come, sit in the stillness
Let my Spirit refill
Every part of your being
Your mind, body, and will

Come, sit in my presence
And my love receive
And know in your heart
That I'll never leave

Come, sit in the solitude
Breathe in my peace
Let go of your fears
Receive my gift of release

> *For God alone my soul waits in silence;*
> *from him comes my salvation.*
> *Psalm 62:1*

A New Beginning

Lord, each day is a new beginning
A wonderful fresh new start
Help me not to feel time is slipping away
Please keep me young and fresh at heart

There are so many things I haven't done yet
I was a late bloomer you know
This can't be the time for winding down
I feel I'm just beginning to go!

So many things I've never tried
For fear of falling flat
I'm tired of being a perfectionist
Let's say goodbye to that!

So, here I am Lord, growing older
Looking ahead down the years
Trusting you each and every step
As together we're conquering my fears

The best is yet to come, Lord
I know that in my heart
Thank you for always being the same
And that each day's a brand new start

Yes, Lord, each day's a new beginning
A new opportunity to grow
Every day I can start all over again
As I live in your Spirit's flow

> *So if anyone is in Christ, there is a new creation:*
> *everything old has passed away;*
> *see, everything has become new!*
>
> *2 Corinthians 5:17*

Meet with Me

There is a price to pay
I know it in my heart
To follow you each day
Lord, help me make a start

Lord, I want to live by grace
I'm tired of living by law
Lord, I want to see your face
To walk through your open door

Lord, I accept your invitation
To meet with you each day
In the morning time or evening quiet
To read your word and to pray

Lord, help me to keep this commitment
I can only do it with you
I've failed so many times before
Please help me to start anew

Lord, fill me with your energy
Morning, noon and night
Help me to relax in you
And not to get so uptight

Lord, I know you want to meet with me
What an amazing thought!
Why do I resist your invitation
To be healed by your love, and taught?

Oh, Lord, the silence is deafening
It's ringing in my ears
How wonderful to hear your voice
To confess to you my fears

Lord, can I really do this
Meet with you every day?
Hear your voice calling to me
And teaching me how to pray?

Yes, my child, I know you can
But only by grace, not by law
I will make it possible
My love into you I'll pour

Come meet with me, my beloved
Many times through your day
Turn to me at every point
I promise to show you the way

I love you so much, my precious one
More than you truly believe
Give yourself to me each day
Open your heart and receive

Simon Peter answered Jesus, "Lord, to whom can we go?
You have the words of eternal life. We have come to
believe and know that you are the Holy One of God."

John 6:68–69

My Prayer Chair

Lord, why am I not sitting in my prayer chair
as I have this conversation with you?
You already know the answer,
So do I
I can't sit in my prayer chair
because it's full to overflowing with stuff
Filled with piles of clothes, and books and plastic bags

Why do I find it so difficult
to keep this particular chair clear of clutter?
To keep it empty, in fact,
So that I can actually use it
for its proper purpose
Not as a dumping ground
but as the special space I've designated,
set apart to sit in
when I want to talk with you
and listen to what you want to say to me

Lord, the piles of things in my prayer chair
prevent me from sitting in it
It reminds me of my overstuffed life,
spilling over
with activities and appointments,
meetings and messages,
voice mail and email

Help me, Lord
to empty my crammed life
of everything
except the things you want me to keep in it
so there is room for you

Help me, Lord
to empty my piled up prayer chair
so there is space for you and me
to sit together and talk

*And after Jesus had dismissed the crowds,
he went up the mountain by himself to pray.*

Matthew 14:23

Do Not Doubt But Believe

If only it could be that simple
Simply to decide to believe
Could it really be that simple
Your gift of faith to receive?

Jesus you said it so clearly
"Do not doubt but believe"
But I need to have my doubts answered
I can't simply let go and believe

It would be too easy
To decide not to doubt at all
To choose to take you at your word
To respond in faith to your call

I've tried so long to figure you out
To get it straight in my head
But I hear you gently calling my name
And asking me to be led

But I want to know where you'll lead me
What will following you cost?
What does a life of faith look like?
Can my doubts just simply be tossed?

Thank you that you understand me
With all of my doubts and my fears
You're letting me know that you love me
That you've loved me through all of these years

You know that this isn't easy
To give up my doubts to you
But I know that you want me to trust you
And to believe what you say is true

So here I am standing before you
Trying so hard to believe
My doubts I lay before you
Your gift of faith I receive

Jesus said to her, "I am the resurrection and the life.
Those who believe in me, even though they die, will live,
and everyone who lives and believes in me will never die.
Do you believe this?"

John 11:25-26

Won't You Come and Dance with Me?

One day I heard Jesus say to me
"Please won't you come and dance with me?"
I couldn't believe he was inviting me
But he used my name and I could see
That he was looking straight at me

He held out his hand and asked again
"Won't you come and dance with me?
I've waited so long for you to respond
To my invitation to dance with me"

"Don't worry that you don't know the steps
I'll teach you, I'll need to
Because the dance is new
You haven't danced this dance before
Just follow my lead
And relax in my arms
I won't let you fall
Or step on my toes
You'll be amazed how gracefully you can dance
When you dance with me
And let me lead"

"So, please, won't you come and dance with me?
I want to heal you and set you free
I know all the steps, you'll see
I can't wait for you to dance with me!"

*And Jesus said to them, "Follow me, and I will make you
fish for people." Immediately they left
their nets and followed him.*

Matthew 4:19–20

The Fern

I see the fresh new fern before my eyes
Curled up, closed like a clenched fist
Almost crippled, bent and twisted in a ball
But as the sun touches it, gently caressing
It begins to unfold, unbend, untwist
It starts to open up its fingery fronds
To receive light and warmth and strength
Gradually it opens
And stretches out its leaves
To embrace life

Lord, I am like the fern
So often I'm closed to your life and light
I am closed to the warmth of your love
I become crippled and bent, twisted
Shutting out you and others
Please shine your light and love on me
Even when I don't seem to want you to
So that your love, often felt through other people
May straighten me out and unbend me
Open me up to your light and love
So that I, too, may reach out and stretch
To embrace life

What has come into being in him was life, and the life was the light of all people. The light shines in the darkness, and the darkness did not overcome it.

John 1:3-5

Wondrous Grace

When you look into God's face
What do you expect to see?
Disapproval? Disappointment?
Anger? Judgment?

I used to fear those expressions
So I avoided looking for God's face
I certainly didn't want to see God looking at me
So I tried to hide
Hide who I knew I was
Because I was sure God wouldn't approve of me

Then one glorious day
I met Jesus Christ
I guess I got to know him gradually
But finally I saw him face to face
And when I looked
I mean, really looked into his face
I was surprised and relieved to see
Nothing but grace
Astonishing, wonderful, unbelievable grace
Astounding, life-changing, lavish grace
Amazingly merciful
Grace

Where was the frown I always feared?
The scowl I had so long dreaded?
The condemnation I expected to hear pronounced?
The sentence I knew I deserved?

And when I look up into his compassionate face
I melt in the warmth of his gift of grace as
I feel the acceptance of his loving embrace
I have come home!

I have never before been in such a place
Surrounded, overwhelmed
With his wondrous grace
Oh, how I long to stay here forever!

So he set off and went to his father. But while he was still
far off, his father saw him and was filled with compassion;
he ran and put his arms around him and kissed him . . . "let
us eat and celebrate; for this son of mine was dead and is
alive again; he was lost and is found!"
And they began to celebrate.
Luke 15:20, 23-24

Overload

Lord, it all seems too much
Another day of drudgery
I can't see the light at the end of the tunnel
I can't seem to get on top of things
Everything feels like it's piling up on top of me

Lord, please help me
Lord, please restore my hope
Give me the energy to face today's challenges
Give me strength and courage
Clear my mind by the power of your Holy Spirit
So that I can discern your priorities
For my time and my attention
Thank you that I move into this new day
With you by my side
That there is nowhere I will go today without you
Help me to rest in that assurance
To rely on you, and not on my own feeble attempts
To be in control
Lord, I long for peace
Teach me how to receive it from you
Along with your gifts of joy and love
Help me to move from this place of despondency and fear
Into the light of trusting you for everything – everything!
Remind me of the truth
That nothing is impossible with you
You want me to greet each new day
With a sense of adventure and expectancy
With joyful anticipation
Of what you are going to do
In and through me this day

Thank you, Lord, for your constancy and your faithfulness
Thank you for always being there
Thank you for this new day
Full of possibilities
Full of hope
Full of life
Full of you
Let me embrace this day as a gift from you
And together we will unwrap it
And discover what joys and surprises it contains!

Likewise the Spirit helps us in our weakness; for we do not know how to pray as we ought, but that very Spirit intercedes with sighs too deep for words.

Romans 8:26

Stop!

Stop!
Stop trying to hold yourself up
Stop trying to do it on your own

You can't be your own support system
You were never intended to be
You need the love, encouragement,
And nurture of other people,
Fellow pilgrims along the way

I am your life-support system
Everything comes from me
Stop trying to do it all on your own

You don't have to produce anything
I am the producer
Of life, love, ideas, energy, ministry, hope,
Healing, tears, laughter and peace

I do the work, yes, sometimes through you,
But I do the work
You're not responsible
For results, success, anything

Except to listen for my voice
To feel my nudges
And to respond, to obey, to act

So, once again, I say to you
Stop trying and striving and struggling
To do it on your own
You can't be a follower of mine on your own,
By yourself in glorious isolation
You need other people
To love you, encourage you, challenge you
To support you, affirm you, confront you

You need other people
To be, with you, my body in my world today
To be an expression of my truth today
To show forth my love today
To my hurting, screaming, torn-apart world
And to give my children
Hope in the midst of despair
Relief in the midst of pain
A spark of light
At the end of a seemingly endless tunnel

I didn't create you to be alone
But to be in relationship,
Sharing your life with others
So, stop!
Stop trying to do it all on your own

Jesus said, "Abide in me as I abide in you.
Just as the branch cannot bear fruit by itself
unless it abides in the vine,
neither can you unless you abide in me.
I am the vine, you are the branches.
Those who abide in me and I in them bear much fruit,
because apart from me you can do nothing."

John 15:4-5

Change

Lord, here I am
Surrounded
Overwhelmed
By all the changes in my life
Which way to turn?
Which path to pursue?
Nothing is permanent
Everything is in turmoil
All seems so uncertain

Lord, I need your help
I need to sense your presence
I need to know the truth
That you are aware of my situation
That you know about the chaos swirling all around me
And within me too

Lord, I want you to be the compass of my life
I need you to be my anchor
In the midst of stormy seas
The haven and sanctuary
When I'm weary and worn
May I hear your gentle voice
In the midst of my confusion
In the midst of all the other voices
Which attempt to distract me
From you, and your ways, and your kingdom

Lord, please show me your next step for me
Step by step, reveal your plan
And purposes for my life
So that I may bring glory to your name
And find joy and fulfillment
In using my gifts to bless others
And in serving my sisters and brothers in your world

Thank you, Lord, that you are the changeless one
That you are always the same
Always trustworthy - worthy of my trust
Always faithful - full of faith and faithfulness
You are the one who keeps your promises
And the one who can be relied upon
May I cling to you, my rock
In the midst of all the choices and changes in my life
Grant me your stability, your peace, your security
So that I can learn all you want me to learn
About trusting and obedience through change

Lord, help me not to resist
The changes that you want me to make
Help me to grow through the changes
That seem forced upon me
Which are out of my control
So that through it all
I can see your hand
Hear your voice
Calling and sending
Guiding and directing
So that I can rest in the knowledge

That you are with me
Through every challenge
And every change
That I have the opportunity to make

May I come to the place
Where I can welcome change
As a friend, not a foe
Embrace it, and learn from it
And at the end of each day, honestly say
Thank you, God, for change

For I the Lord do not change

Malachi 3:6

Hold On To Hope

How do we hold on to hope
In the midst of suffering and pain?
By holding on to Jesus
And by calling upon his name

How do we hold on to hope
In the face of chaos and death?
By holding on to Jesus
And by thanking God for each breath

How do we hold on to hope
When overwhelmed by grief and despair?
By holding on to Jesus
As we reach out with loving care

How do we hold on to hope
In the midst of our fear and our loss?
By holding on to Jesus
And keeping our eyes on the cross

How do we hold on to hope
And encourage each other to love?
By holding on to Jesus
Who gives us his peace from above

May the God of hope fill you with all joy and peace in
believing, so that you may abound in hope
by the power of the Holy Spirit.

Romans 15:13

Start Trusting

I need to write, but I don't know what to say
I need to live, but what shall I do with the day?
I need to scream, but all I can manage is a silent cry
Why am I letting life pass me by?

Once again I ask you, Lord
Where does all this anger and confusion come from?
These hateful, seething feelings
And recurring resentments?
Why can't I bury the hatred, let go of the anger?
You came to rescue and redeem
Must I always play the tapes in my head
With the same old negative themes?

You came to help me Lord
Why do I find it all so difficult?
Why do I always want to make mountains
Out of molehills?
How can I be so immature and fragile?
So petty and perverse
So selfish and so full of self-pity

Shake me free from all these chains, Jesus
All these ropes that bind my feet
Why can't I leap into your light?
Jump into your joy?
Abandon myself to your attitudes?
Give myself to your game plan?
Surrender myself to your Spirit?

Life would be far simpler if you'd do that
Stop trying and start trusting me
Don't you believe that I love you
And that my desire is to set you free?
I know you've heard it so often
But this time I'm telling you
Give all of yourself to me
And you'll prove that my word is true

Therefore, since we are surrounded by so great a cloud of witnesses, let us also lay aside every weight and the sin that clings so closely, and let us run with perseverance the race that is set before us, looking to Jesus the pioneer and perfecter of our faith.

Hebrews 12:1-2

What Will Fill My Emptiness?

What will fill my emptiness?
I asked myself one day
Money? Power? A beautiful home?
Shopping? Or games to play?

What will fill my emptiness?
I asked my friend one day
Food or travel? Success at work?
She said, "I suggest you pray"

What will fill my emptiness?
I asked Jesus Christ one day
"Not all the stuff you're acquiring"
I heard him gently say

Then what will fill my emptiness?
I asked him once again
I want to learn contentment
But I don't know how to begin

"Put God first in everything"
Came back his quick reply
"And do exactly what God says
Even when you don't know why"

"Let God fill you with his love
And learn to trust God's will
When you obey, his peace and joy
Your emptiness will fill"

What will fill my emptiness?
I ask myself today
Holy Spirit, please show me
As I learn to trust and obey

*I pray that you may have the power to comprehend, with
all the saints, what is the breadth and length and height
and depth, and to know the love of Christ that
surpasses knowledge, so that you may be filled
with all the fullness of God.*

Ephesians 3:18-19

Lord, Teach Me

Lord, teach me, please teach me
There's so much I need to learn
Lord, love me, please love me
For your grace I yearn

Lord, heal me, please heal me
I have so much pain
Lord, touch me, please touch me
And make me whole again

Lord, talk to me, please talk to me
I need to hear your voice
Lord, guide me, please guide me
Help me make the right choice

Lord, hold me, please hold me
So that the healing can start
Lord, fill me, please fill me
And mend my hurting heart

Lord, whisper, speak
Yes, shout if you need
To get me to listen
And your voice to heed
Once again you are challenging me

Listen to me, if you want to be freed
There's no other way
To the healing you need
No short cuts, or quick fixes
But my words you must heed
If you want the new life
To which I will lead

Teach me your way, O Lord,
that I may walk in your truth;
give me an undivided heart to revere your name.
I give thanks to you, O Lord my God, with my whole heart,
and I will glorify your name forever.

Psalm 86:11-12

Choose Life!

Many years ago
I wished that I was dead
How did such a crazy thought
Ever creep into my head?

In those days I didn't know
How much God thinks I'm worth
That God would send his only Son
To come to live on earth

Jesus tells us of God's love
And how we can be forgiven
He shows us how to love each other
And how we can experience heaven

Because of God's amazing grace
Instead of you and me
Jesus Christ was willing to die
By being crucified on a tree

By his death, our life was won
Now and for eternity
Accept, my friend, what Jesus has done
To forgive and set you free

So today, my friend, choose life!
For your life is a gift from God
Believe today how precious you are
Yes, you are the one God loves!

Jesus said, "And this is eternal life, that they may know
you, the only true God, and Jesus Christ
whom you have sent."
John 17:3

A New Day

Today is a new day!
It has never been lived before
This day is full of potential
What will I use it for?

This day is a new day!
A gift from the Father above
Lord, I want to use this day for you
Please fill me with your love

Today is a new day!
May your grace make me brand new
Fill me with your Spirit, Lord
As I listen for direction from you

This day is a new day!
Lord, open my eyes and heart
So that I can see as you see
Fill me with hope as I start

Today is a new day!
Yesterday is gone
May I live today with faith and joy
As I sing its special song

Jesus said, "I give you a new commandment,
that you love one another.
Just as I have loved you, you also should love one another."

John 13:34

Beyond Myself

Lord, please show me
How to get beyond myself
Everywhere I go – I am there
Thank you God that so are you!
Help me to understand
How to die to myself
How to forget myself
By giving all of me to you

When I fear that I will be lost
Forgotten forever
If I relinquish control to you
Remind me in your gentle whisper
That this is the only way to find myself
By losing myself in you
Not in another human being
You're the only one who can be trusted with my whole life
All of me, all of who I am now, all of who I am becoming
And all that you are calling me to be

Help me to trust you, loving Lord
With more of me, more of my life
So that each day I may surrender
More of myself to you
Thereby discovering more of your life in me

Then Jesus said to them all, "If any want to become my followers, let them deny themselves and take up their cross daily and follow me. For those who want to save their life will lose it, and those who lose their life for my sake will save it. What does it profit them if they gain the whole world, but lose or forfeit themselves?"

Luke 9:23-25

The Challenge

Lord, this is the biggest challenge of my life!
I can only do it if it is your will
It's incredible how far you've brought me
Yet it's so easy to resist you still

I can hardly believe what's happening to me
The changes ahead loom so large
It's scary and exciting to step out in faith
I must trust you're the one who's in charge

You've spoken directly once again
To my waiting, listening heart
There's no denying your message this time
A new adventure's about to start

Lord, help me not to be afraid
To trust you at every turn
To know that your Spirit's within me
Empowering me and helping me learn

Do not fear, for I am with you,
do not be afraid, for I am your God;
I will strengthen you, I will help you,
I will uphold you with my victorious right hand.

Isaiah 41:10

An Unopened Gift

Lord, I am an unopened gift
So often I am closed
To you, to others
Even to myself

Open me up, Lord
but please do it gently
Because there are things inside of me
that I don't want to discover
or acknowledge that they exist—
        ugly, angry, unpleasant things

Help me, Lord, to look at those parts of who I am
that need the searchlight of your righteous love
that need the cleansing of your redeeming grace
that need the washing of your forgiving mercy
that need the healing of your restoring love

But, thank God, that's not all that's inside of me!

Thank you, Lord, that you want to open me up
to set free all the wonderful things inside the gift that is me
my unique personality
my talents and abilities
gifts from you to me and now my gifts to others
which is a way of giving back to you
everything that makes me, me!
my smile, my laughter, my voice
the ways people recognize me

Lord, please help me to open up
and to unpack the gift of who I am
to unwrap the gift of my life
and to discover, day by day
who you are calling me to be
and what you are asking me to do for you

Then I will be able to participate more fully in life
and be able to celebrate more joyfully
the gifts that I have received from you
and the gifts you want me to share with your world
as I open up the gift that is me

Now to him who by the power at work within us is able to accomplish abundantly far more than all we can ask or imagine, to him be glory in the church and in Christ Jesus to all generations, forever and ever. Amen.

Ephesians 3:20–21

Self Acceptance

Accept myself?
What a concept
Lord, would it be alright to do that?
To accept myself?
But what about my flaws, my mistakes, my sins?
How can I possibly accept all of that?

You know that I feel a constant push to improve,
To do better, to do more
Where does that push come from?
Does it come from you, Lord, or from other people,
Or from inside myself?

Help me, Lord, to receive your vote of confidence
Your acceptance of me – imperfections and all
If I were perfect, well, and whole
There would have been no need for you to come to earth
You know only too well
How broken I am
How much I need your help and healing
How much I need your strength, your power,
Your Spirit, your life, living in me

Lord, this day, help me to accept where I am
At this point in my life
Deliver me from the curse of always feeling
That I ought to be someone else, somewhere else

Doing better, farther ahead
Feeling that I'm still trying to catch up
Thinking that I'm somehow failing you and myself
Help me to choose to stop entertaining those thoughts
And to accept that I am where I am - today
To accept that I am who you created me to be
So that I can relax, let go of the pressure
Silence the demanding voices in my head
And simply be me
What a relief that would be!

*For it was you who formed my inward parts; you knit me
together in my mother's womb.
I praise you, for I am fearfully and wonderfully made.
Wonderful are your works;
that I know very well.*

Psalm 139:13–14

Jesus, Remember Me

Jesus, remember me
When you come into your kingdom

Oh, my precious one
It isn't me who forgets,
Who needs to remember you!
I never forget you
Not even for a moment

You are the one who forgets me
You are the one who needs
To remember me!

Think how frequently you forget me
How easily you forget me
How often you need reminding
To remember me

I am not the one who forgets
I'm not the one with memory loss
You are
Please remember me during your hectic day
Remember me
I never forget you
Never
I always remember you
Always, always
I always love you
Always, always

*Jesus said, "And remember, I am with you always,
to the end of the age."*

Matthew 28:20

I am Loved!

I am loved
I am beautiful
I am happy to be me
I am lovable
I am forgiven
How amazing it is to begin to love me!

Jesus loves me, he really does!
And now I'm choosing to believe it's true
If you ask me why I never could before
Pride and inferiority will give you a clue

It's wonderful to feel a new peace inside
To stop struggling to try and change me
I'm letting the transformation happen
God's the only one who can remake you and me

I have called you by name, you are mine. . .
you are precious in my sight, and honored, and I love you.

Isaiah 43:1,4

Let Go! Let Go!

Let go and believe
Let go and receive
My deep, deep love for you

Let go and receive
Let go and believe
That you can be made anew

Let go and step out
Step out in my love
Relax in this new way of living
Let go of your fears
That you've held onto for years
And practice my way of forgiving

Let go! Let go!
Let me live my life through you
I know you still resist me
Let go! Let go!
Stop trying to control everyone else and me
Letting go will help set you free

Let go of hate and jealousy too
Let go of anger and resentment
Make room for love and peace and joy
Room for forgiveness and contentment

Let go! Let go!
Just as you would a rope
Let go! and receive
My blessings, faith and hope

Why am I so afraid that I'll fall?
Afraid that I cannot hear your call
Help me, Lord to trust you more
Your peace into my heart please pour

Lord, I want to trust you more
I'm so glad you don't keep score
Of all the times I've let you down
I don't need to fear your frown

You are loving and full of grace
You look at me with a smiling face
And graciously once more you say
        Let go! Let go!
        Let go! – today!

Therefore, since we are justified by faith, we have peace
with God through our Lord Jesus Christ, through whom
we have obtained access to this grace in which we stand

Romans 5:1–2

Give Me Everything

Give me everything
I heard God say
Give it all to me
God simply said to me one day

How can I do that?
I asked God in reply
I know that I need to
Or I will surely die

How do I give you all my stuff
My lies, my fears, my sin?
Open up your hands and heart
And let my love flow in

Let go of your pain, your hurt, your regrets
Relinquish to me your hopes and your dreams
Let go of resentment and unforgiveness too
Stop trying to manipulate, give up your schemes

Give me all your lack of trust
All your pride and envy too
For as you give me everything
Your whole being I will renew

*For surely I know the plans I have for you, says the Lord,
plans for your welfare and not for harm,
to give you a future with hope.*

Jeremiah 29:11

Free!

Oh the joy of becoming free
Oh the joy of being me
Lord, you're setting me free indeed
You forgive me and love me
You know all my need
You know how much I long to be freed

You hear my deepest cries of pain
You answer me and call my name
Sometimes I don't believe that I can be free
I think I always have to stay the same
But you open my eyes so that I can see
The woman of faith you are calling me to be

Then Jesus said . . . "If you continue in my word, you are truly my disciples; and you will know the truth, and the truth will make you free. So if the Son makes you free, you will be free indeed."

John 8:31-32, 36

My Gift

This is my gift to you, my child
Open your heart to receive it
This is my gift to you, my beloved one
More than you could ever ask or hope for
I know exactly what you need
Better than you do yourself
So open your heart, open your hands
Receive my gift of love for you
Receive my grace and forgiveness too
Let go of fear, of doubt and pain
I want you to learn to be a child again
Learn to live in the freedom of my care
There is no need for anxiety there
Learn how to trust, to hope, to laugh
I am with you along life's path
Learn how to give with all your heart
Without any fear you'll be torn apart
Learn how to risk, to face the unknown
Learn how to praise, not complain and moan
Learn how to forgive, how to show mercy too
For as you know, no one's worse than you
Learn from me the secrets of life
Know peace and joy, not anger and strife

Know that I'm there at every turn
I'm always available for you to learn
How to be and how to do
Exactly what I'm asking you to
Step by step, learn from me
Step by step, becoming free
Know my love, I'm there for you
I'm always there to carry you through
Accept this gift from me to you
And know in your heart my love is true

Every generous act of giving, with every perfect gift, is from above, coming down from the Father of lights, with whom there is no variation or shadow due to change.

James 1:17

Something New

Lord, please do something new
Do something new in me
Lord, I need something new
So that I can be truly free

Lord, I don't know what I need
But thank you that you do
You want me to be healed and freed
Lord, please show me something new

Lord, let me hear your voice anew
Speaking right to me
Lord, please tell me something new
That will unbind and set me free

Thank you, Lord, that you never stop
Doing something new
Every day, like a brand new crop
You're creating something new

Help me, Lord, to let go of the old
To make space for all that's new
Help me, Lord, to risk and be bold
And be open to something new!

> *Do not remember the former things,*
> *or consider the things of old.*
> *I am about to do a new thing;*
> *now it springs forth, do you not perceive it?*
>
> *Isaiah 43:18-19*

Thank You

There is so much, Lord, to thank you for
Thank you for life and breath
Thank you for friends, for love
For family, work, and faith

"Thank you" seems such an inadequate expression
For all the gifts you shower upon me
Day in, and day out.
Even when I don't mention my gratitude to you
You continue to pour your love and grace into my life.
When I forget or ignore you
You don't suddenly withdraw
Or withhold your gracious gifts.
Your patience and faithfulness
Your loving kindness
Astound me

Lord, please shake me out of my complacency
When I cease to be amazed
And stunned by your grace
By your endless mercy
By your unfathomable love

Help me, Lord, to live my life
Overflowing with thankfulness to you
And full of gratitude
For all your incredible grace

I will give thanks to the Lord with my whole heart;
I will tell of all your wonderful deeds.
Psalm 9:1–2

Additional Scriptures
(NRSV)

Frantic Pace

The Lord bless you and keep you; the Lord make his face
to shine upon you, and be gracious to you; the Lord lift up
his countenance upon you, and give you peace.
Numbers 6:24-26

O taste and see that the Lord is good; happy are those who
take refuge in him.
Psalm 34:8

How sweet are your words to my taste, sweeter than
honey to my mouth!
Psalm 119:103

And the Word became flesh and lived among us, and we
have seen his glory . . . full of grace and truth.
John 1:14

Be Still and Know that I Am God

The Lord is good to those who wait for him,
to the soul that seeks him.
It is good that one should wait quietly
for the salvation of the Lord.
Lamentations 3:25-26

Six days shall work be done; but the seventh day is a
sabbath of complete rest.
Leviticus 23:3

"Be still, and know that I am God!
I am exalted among the nations, I am exalted in the earth."

The Lord of hosts is with us; the God of
Jacob is our refuge.
Psalm 46:10-11

But I have calmed and quieted my soul,
like a weaned child with its mother.
Psalm 131:2

Come, Sit in My Presence

For God alone my soul waits in silence; from him comes
my salvation. He alone is my rock and my salvation,
my fortress; I shall never be shaken.
Psalm 62:1-2

Be still before the Lord, and wait patiently for him.
Psalm 37:7

For thus said the Lord God, the Holy One of Israel: In
returning and rest you shall be saved; in quietness and in
trust shall be your strength.
Isaiah 30:15

Jesus said, "Peace I leave with you; my peace I give to
you. I do not give to you as the world gives. Do not let
your hearts be troubled, and do not let them be afraid."
John 14:27

A New Beginning

So if anyone is in Christ, there is a new creation: everything old has passed away; see,
everything has become new!
2 Corinthians 5:17

He put a new song in my mouth,
a song of praise to our God.
Psalm 40:3

Blessed be the God and Father of our Lord Jesus Christ!
By his great mercy he has given us
a new birth into a living hope through
the resurrection of Jesus Christ from the dead.
1 Peter 1:3

Meet with Me

Simon Peter answered Jesus, "Lord, to whom can we go?
You have the words of eternal life. We have come to
believe and know that you are the Holy One of God."
John 6:68

Listen to my voice, and do all that I command you. So
shall you be my people, and I will be your God.
Jeremiah 11:4

The law indeed was given through Moses; grace and truth
came through Jesus Christ.
John 1:17

Jesus said, "Listen! I am standing at the door, knocking; if
you hear my voice and open the door, I will come in to
you and eat with you, and you with me."
Revelation 3:20

My Prayer Chair

And after Jesus had dismissed the crowds, he went up the
mountain by himself to pray.
Matthew 14:23

Let us therefore approach the throne of grace with
boldness, so that we may receive mercy
and find grace to help in time of need.
Hebrews 4:16

Jesus said, "So I say to you, Ask, and it will be given you;
search, and you will find; knock, and the door will be
opened for you."
Luke 11:9

Do not worry about anything, but in everything by prayer
and supplication with thanksgiving
let your requests be made known to God. And the peace
of God, which surpasses all understanding,
will guard your hearts and your minds in Christ Jesus.
Philippians 4:6-7

Do Not Doubt But Believe

Jesus said to her, "I am the resurrection and the life. Those
who believe in me, even though they die, will live, and
everyone who lives and believes in me will never die.
Do you believe this?"
John 11:25-26

Jesus said, "The time is fulfilled, and the kingdom of God
has come near; repent, and believe in the good news."
Mark 1:15

Jesus said, "For God so loved the world that he gave his
only Son, so that everyone who believes in him may not
perish but may have eternal life."
John 3:16

Then Jesus said to Thomas, "Put your finger here and see
my hands. Reach out your hand and put it in my side. Do

not doubt but believe." Thomas answered him, "My Lord
and my God!" Jesus said to him, "Have you believed
because you have seen me?
Blessed are those who have not seen
and yet have come to believe."
John 20:27-29

Won't You Come and Dance with Me?

As Jesus walked by the Sea of Galilee, he saw two brothers, Simon, who is called Peter, and Andrew his brother,
casting a net into the sea – for they were fishermen.
And he said to them, "Follow me, and I will make you
fish for people." Immediately they
left their nets and followed him.
Matthew 4:18-20

As Jesus was walking along, he saw a man called Matthew
sitting at the tax booth; and he said to him, "Follow me."
And he got up and followed him.
Matthew 9:9

The Fern

In the beginning was the Word, and the Word was with
God, and the Word was God. He was in the beginning
with God. All things came into being through him, and
without him not one thing came into being. What has
come into being in him was life, and the life was the light
of all people. The light shines in the darkness, and the
darkness did not overcome it.
John 1:1-5

Again Jesus spoke to them, saying, "I am the light of the
world. Whoever follows me will never walk in darkness
but will have the light of life."
John 8:12

Jesus said to him, "I am the way,
and the truth, and the life. No one comes to the Father
except through me."
John 14:6

And this is the testimony: God gave us eternal life, and
this life is in his Son. Whoever has the Son has life;
whoever does not have the Son of God does not have life.
1 John 5:11-12

Wondrous Grace

So he set off and went to his father. But while he was still
far off, his father saw him and was filled with compassion;
he ran and put his arms around him and kissed him . . .
"let us eat and celebrate; for this son of mine was dead and
is alive again; he was lost and is found!"
And they began to celebrate.
Luke 15:20, 23-24

Jesus said, "If you know me, you will know my Father
also. From now on you do know him and have seen him."
John 14:7

the surpassing grace of God that he has given you. Thanks
be to God for his indescribable gift!
2 Corinthians 9:14-15

In him we have redemption through his blood, the forgiveness of our trespasses, according to the riches of his grace
that he lavished on us.
Ephesians 1:7-8

Overload

Likewise the Spirit helps us in our weakness; for we do
not know how to pray as we ought, but that very Spirit
intercedes with sighs too deep for words.
Romans 8:26

Answer me quickly, O Lord; my spirit fails.
Do not hide your face from me,
or I shall be like those who go down to the Pit.
Let me hear of your steadfast love in the morning,
for in you I put my trust.
Teach me the way I should go,
for to you I lift up my soul.
Psalm 143:7-8

Have you not known? Have you not heard? The Lord is
the everlasting God, the Creator of the ends
of the earth. He does not faint or grow weary;
his understanding is unsearchable. He gives power to the
faint, and strengthens the powerless.
Even youths will faint and be weary, and the
young will fall exhausted;
but those who wait for the Lord
shall renew their strength, they shall mount up with wings
like eagles, they shall run and not be weary,
they shall walk and not faint.
Isaiah 40:28-31

Jesus said, "My grace is sufficient for you, for my
power is made perfect in weakness."
2 Corinthians 12:9

Stop!

Jesus said, "Abide in me as I abide in you. Just as the
branch cannot bear fruit by itself unless it abides in the
vine, neither can you unless you abide in me.
I am the vine, you are the branches. Those who abide in
me and I in them bear much fruit, because apart from me
you can do nothing."
John 15:4-5

For as in one body we have many members,
and not all the members have the same function, so we,
who are many, are one body in Christ,
and individually we are members one of another.
Romans 12:4-5

Therefore encourage one another and
build up each other, as indeed you are doing.
1 Thessalonians 5:11

Change

For I the Lord do not change.
Malachi 3:6

Jesus Christ is the same yesterday and today and forever.
Hebrews 13:8

Hold On To Hope

May the God of hope fill you with all joy and peace in
believing, so that you may abound in hope
by the power of the Holy Spirit.
Romans 15:13

I pray that the God of our Lord Jesus Christ, the Father of glory, may give you a spirit of wisdom and revelation as you come to know him, so that, with the eyes of your heart enlightened, you may know what is the hope to which he has called you, what are the riches of his glorious inheritance among the saints, and what is the immeasurable greatness of his power for us who believe, according to the working of his great power.
Ephesians 1:17-19

Now may our Lord Jesus Christ himself and God our Father, who loved us and through grace gave us eternal comfort and good hope, comfort your hearts and strengthen them in every good work and word.
2 Thessalonians 2:16-17

We have this hope, a sure and steadfast anchor of the soul.
Hebrews 6:19

Start Trusting

Therefore, since we are surrounded by so great a cloud of witnesses, let us also lay aside every weight and the sin that clings so closely, and let us run with perseverance the race that is set before us, looking to Jesus the pioneer and perfecter of our faith, who for the sake of the joy that was set before him endured the cross, disregarding its shame, and has taken his seat at the right hand of the throne of God.
Hebrews 12:1-2

Trust in him at all times, O people; pour out your heart before him; God is a refuge for us.
Psalm 62:8

Trust in the Lord with all your heart,
and do not rely on your own insight. In all
your ways acknowledge him, and he will make straight
your paths. Do not be wise in your own eyes; fear the
Lord, and turn away from evil. It will be a healing for
your flesh and a refreshment for your body.
Proverbs 3:5-8

Blessed are those who trust in the Lord,
whose trust is the Lord.
They shall be like a tree planted by water,
sending out its roots by the stream. It shall not fear when
heat comes, and its leaves shall stay green;
in the year of drought
it is not anxious, and it does not cease to bear fruit.
Jeremiah 17:7-8

What Will Fill My Emptiness?

I pray that you may have the power to comprehend with
all the saints, what is the breadth and length and height
and depth and to know the love of Christ
that surpasses knowledge, so that you may
be filled with all the fullness of God.
Ephesians 3:18-19

You show me the path of life.
In your presence there is fullness of joy;
in your right hand are pleasures forevermore.
Psalm 16:11

From his fullness we have all received, grace upon grace.
John 1:16

Jesus said to her, "Everyone who drinks
of this water will be thirsty again,
but those who drink of the water that
I will give them will never be thirsty.
The water that I will give will become in them a spring
of water gushing up to eternal life."
John 4:13-14

Lord, Teach Me

Teach me your way, O Lord, that I may walk in your truth;
give me an undivided heart
to revere your name. I give thanks to you,
O Lord my God, with my whole heart, and I will glorify
your name forever.
Psalm 86:11-12

Make me to know your ways, O Lord;
teach me your paths. Lead me in your truth, and teach me,
for you are the God of my salvation;
for you I wait all day long.
Psalm 25:4-5

Jesus said, "But the Advocate, the Holy Spirit, whom the
Father will send in my name, will teach you everything,
and remind you of all that I have said to you."
John 14:26

Choose Life!

Jesus said, "And this is eternal life, that they may know
you, the only true God, and
Jesus Christ whom you have sent."
John 17:3

I call heaven and earth to witness against you today that I
have set before you life and death,
blessings and curses. Choose life so that you
and your descendants may live, loving the Lord your God,
obeying him, and holding fast to him;
for that means life to you and length of days, so that you
may live in the land that the Lord swore to give to your
ancestors, to Abraham, to Isaac, and to Jacob.
Deuteronomy 30:19-20

Jesus said, "I came that they may have life,
and have it abundantly."
John 10:10

A New Day

Jesus said, "I give you a new commandment,
that you love one another. Just as I have loved you,
you also should love one another."
John 13:34

But this I call to mind, and therefore I have hope:
The steadfast love of the Lord never ceases,
his mercies never come to an end; they are new every
morning; great is your faithfulness.
Lamentations 3:21-23

Beyond Myself

Then Jesus said to them all, "If any want to become my
followers, let them deny themselves
and take up their cross daily and follow me.
For those who want to save their life will lose it,
and those who lose their life for my sake will save it.

What does it profit them if they gain the whole world,
but lose or forfeit themselves?"
Luke 9:23-25

The Challenge

Do not fear, for I am with you, do not be afraid,
for I am your God; I will strengthen you, I will help you, I
will uphold you with my victorious right hand.
Isaiah 41:10

Now faith is the assurance of things hoped for,
the conviction of things not seen.
Hebrews 11:1

An Unopened Gift

Now to him who by the power at work within us is able to
accomplish abundantly far more than all we can ask or
imagine, to him be glory in the church and in Christ Jesus
to all generations, forever and ever. Amen.
Ephesians 3:20

There is therefore now no condemnation for those who are
in Christ Jesus. For the law of the Spirit of life in Christ
Jesus has set you free from the law of sin and death.
Romans 8:1-2

Self Acceptance

For it was you who formed my inward parts; you knit me
together in my mother's womb. I praise you, for I am
fearfully and wonderfully made. Wonderful are your
works; that I know very well. My frame was not hidden
from you, when I was being made in secret, intricately
woven in the depths of the earth.

Your eyes beheld my unformed substance.
In your book were written all the days
that were formed for me,
when none of them as yet existed.
Psalm 139:13-16

Jesus, Remember Me

Jesus said, "And remember, I am with you always,
to the end of the age."
Matthew 28:20

Then he said, "Jesus, remember me when
you come into your kingdom." Jesus replied, "Truly I tell
you, today you will be with me in Paradise."
Luke 23:42–43

I am Loved!

But now thus says the Lord, he who created you,
O Jacob, he who formed you, O Israel:
Do not fear, for I have redeemed you; I have called you by
name, you are mine. . .
you are precious in my sight, and honored, and I love you.
Isaiah 43:1, 4

I have loved you with an everlasting love; therefore I have
continued my faithfulness to you.
Jeremiah 31:3

Jesus said, "As the Father has loved me, so I
have loved you; abide in my love."
John 15:9

But God proves his love for us in that while we still were
sinners Christ died for us.
Romans 5:8

Let Go! Let Go!

Therefore, since we are justified by faith, we have peace
with God through our Lord Jesus Christ, through whom
we have obtained access to this grace in which we stand.
Romans 5:1–2

Jesus said, "My sheep hear my voice. I know them, and
they follow me. I give them eternal life, and they will
never perish. No one will snatch them out of my hand."
John 10:27-28

Give Me Everything

For surely I know the plans I have for you, says the Lord,
plans for your welfare and not for harm, to give you a
future with hope. Then when you call upon me and come
and pray to me, I will hear you. When you search for me,
you will find me; if you seek me with all your heart, I will
let you find me, says the Lord.
Jeremiah 29:11-14

Free!

Then Jesus said, "If you continue in my word, you are
truly my disciples; and you will know the truth,
and the truth will make you free. So if the Son makes
you free, you will be free indeed."
John 8:31-32, 36

Let it be known to you . . . that through this man forgiveness of sins is proclaimed to you; by this Jesus everyone
who believes is set free from all those sins from which you
could not be freed by the law of Moses.
Acts 13:38-39

My Gift

Every generous act of giving, with every perfect gift, is
from above, coming down from the Father of lights, with
whom there is no variation or shadow due to change.
James 1:17

At that time the disciples came to Jesus and asked,
"Who is the greatest in the kingdom of heaven?" He
called a child, whom he put among them, and said, "Truly
I tell you, unless you change and become like children,
you will never enter the kingdom of heaven. Whoever
becomes humble like this child is the greatest in the
kingdom of heaven. Whoever welcomes
one such child in my name welcomes me."
Matthew 18:1-4

And be kind to one another, tenderhearted, forgiving one
another, as God in Christ has forgiven you.
Ephesians 4:32

Cast all your anxiety on him, because he cares for you.
1 Peter 5:7

Something New

Do not remember the former things, or consider the things
of old. I am about to do a new thing; now it springs forth,
do you not perceive it?
Isaiah 43:18-19

A new heart I will give you, and a new spirit I will put
within you; and I will remove from your body the
heart of stone and give you a heart of flesh.
Ezekiel 36:26

Jesus said, "No one sews a piece of unshrunk cloth on an old cloak, for the patch pulls away from the cloak, and a worse tear is made. Neither is new wine put into old wineskins; otherwise, the skins burst, and the wine is spilled, and the skins are destroyed; but new wine is put into fresh wineskins, and so both are preserved."
Matthew 9:16-17

And the one who was seated on the throne said, "See, I am making all things new."
Revelation 21:5

Thank You

I will give thanks to the Lord with my whole heart; I will tell of all your wonderful deeds. I will be glad and exalt in you; I will sing praise to your name, O Most High.
Psalm 9:1–2

O give thanks to the Lord, for he is good; for his steadfast love endures forever.
1 Chronicles 16:34

Giving thanks to God the Father at all times and for everything in the name of our Lord Jesus Christ.
Ephesians 5:20

Rejoice always, pray without ceasing, give thanks in all circumstances; for this is the will of God in Christ Jesus for you.
1 Thessalonians 5:16–18